12/15

PISCES

Lorraine Harrison

PowerKiDS press.

New York

Published in 2016 by The Rosen Publishing Group, Inc.
29 East 21st Street, New York, NY 10010

First Edition

Editor: Katie Kawa
Book Design: Katelyn Heinle

Photo Credits: Cover Yganko/Shutterstock.com; back cover, p. 1 nienora/Shutterstock.com; p. 5 Digital Storm/Shutterstock.com; pp. 6, 7, 14 angelinast/Shutterstock.com; p. 8 http://upload.wikimedia.org/wikipedia/commons/d/d9/Sidney_Hall_-_Urania%27s_Mirror_-_Pisces.jpg; p. 9 eFesenko/Shutterstock.com; p. 11 Fanatic Studio/Getty Images; p. 13 © iStockphoto.com/stevecoleimages; p. 15 Artens/Shutterstock.com; p. 17 Standret/Shutterstock.com; p. 19 Hollygraphic/Shutterstock.com; p. 21 AZSTARMAN/Shutterstock.com; p. 22 Christophe Lehenaff/Photononstop/Getty Images.

Library of Congress Cataloging-in-Publication Data

Harrison, Lorraine, 1959- author.
 Pisces / Lorraine Harrison.
    pages cm. — (The constellation collection)
 Includes bibliographical references and index.
 ISBN 978-1-4994-0935-2 (pbk.)
 ISBN 978-1-4994-0957-4 (6 pack)
 ISBN 978-1-4994-0996-3 (library binding)
 1. Constellations—Juvenile literature. 2. Constellations—Folklore—Juvenile literature. 3. Galaxies—Juvenile literature. 4. Pisces (Constellation)—Juvenile literature. I. Title.
 QB803.H37 2016
 523.1'12—dc23
                            2015009362

Manufactured in the United States of America

CPSIA Compliance Information: Batch #WS15PK: For Further Information contact Rosen Publishing, New York, New York at 1-800-237-9932

CONTENTS

FLYING FISH!

Everyone knows fish live in water. Pisces, however, isn't like other fish. It lives in the stars!

Pisces isn't a real fish. It's actually a constellation, or a group of stars that form the shape of a person, animal, or thing. Pisces, which is sometimes called the Fish, is shaped like a pair of fish joined by a ribbon or **cord**. Lines of stars form the fish and the cord joining them. This makes a shape that looks like a V that's been turned on its side in the sky. People have been studying these fish in the sky for thousands of years.

STAR STORY

Pisces is found in an area of the sky near other water constellations, including Aquarius, which is also known as the Water Bearer.

THE TWO FISH THAT MAKE UP PISCES ARE AT EITHER END OF THE V.

PISCES AND PEGASUS

Pisces can be seen in the sky in both the Northern and the Southern **Hemispheres**. In the Northern Hemisphere, Pisces is most easily seen in fall.

To find Pisces, look for the Great Square of Pegasus, which is part of the Pegasus constellation. This is a square made up of four stars. Below the Great Square of Pegasus is the Circlet of Pisces. This is a ring of stars that forms the head of one of the fish in Pisces. Tracing the line of stars to the left of the Circlet will allow you to find the rest of the constellation.

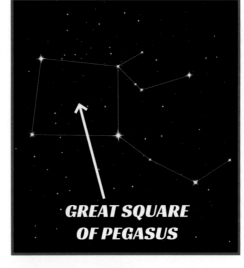

GREAT SQUARE OF PEGASUS

STAR STORY

The second fish in the Pisces constellation can be found by tracing the line of stars upward from the point in the constellation's main V shape. It looks as if this fish is leaping toward the Great Square of Pegasus.

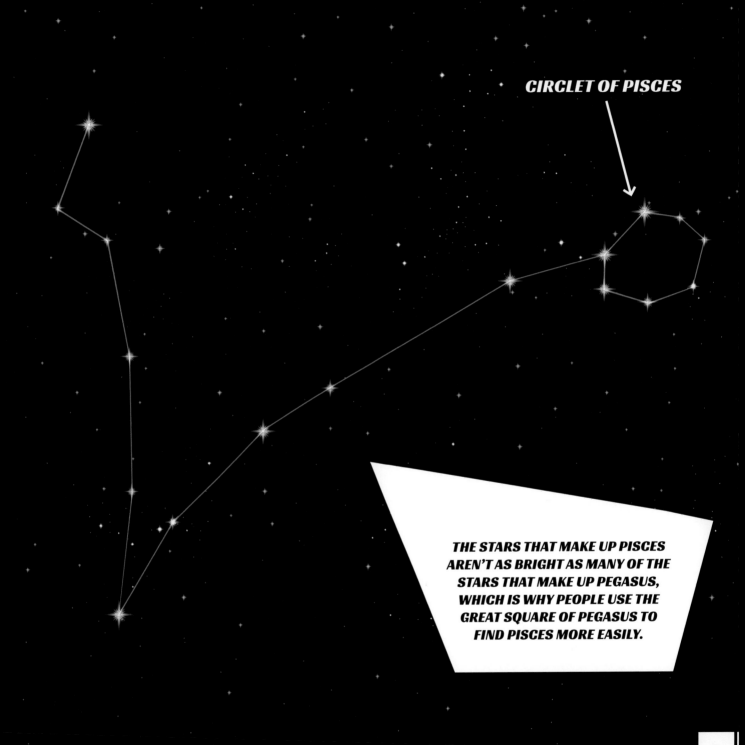

CIRCLET OF PISCES

THE STARS THAT MAKE UP PISCES AREN'T AS BRIGHT AS MANY OF THE STARS THAT MAKE UP PEGASUS, WHICH IS WHY PEOPLE USE THE GREAT SQUARE OF PEGASUS TO FIND PISCES MORE EASILY.

THE STORY OF PISCES

Different groups of ancient people told different **myths** about how two fish came to be in the sky. To the ancient Greeks, the two fish of Pisces represented, or stood for, the goddess Aphrodite and her son Eros.

THE CORD THAT KEPT APHRODITE AND EROS TOGETHER AS THEY SWAM AWAY FROM TYPHOON IS AN IMPORTANT PART OF THE PISCES CONSTELLATION AND CAN BE CLEARLY SEEN IN THIS STAR CHART.

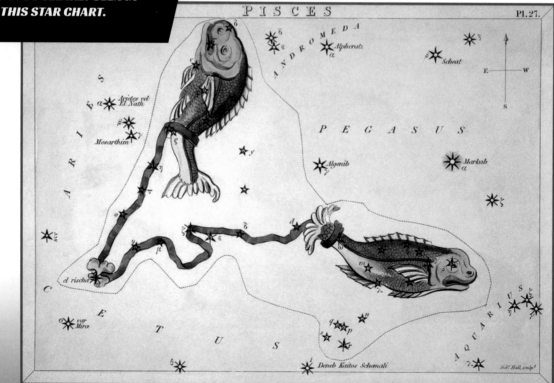

Aphrodite turned herself and Eros into fish in order to escape from a giant monster named Typhoon. This monster attacked Mount Olympus, which was the home of the Greek gods. Each god then turned into an animal to escape Typhoon. Aphrodite and Eros tied their tails together so they wouldn't lose each other.

MOUNT OLYMPUS

STAR STORY

Typhoon was said to be so large that his wings blocked out the sun. The ancient Greeks believed his body was covered in serpents, or snakes, and he could make fiery rocks shoot out of his mouth!

A ZODIAC CONSTELLATION

Pisces is part of the zodiac, which is an imaginary band of signs in the sky that forms a circle around Earth. The signs are based on constellations.

The zodiac is the basis for astrology, which is the belief that the movements of the stars and **planets** affect life on Earth. Some people believe that the position of the planets and constellations on the day a person is born **determines** what their **personality** and life will be like. Each zodiac sign is said to govern a certain time of the year. Pisces governs the time period from around February 19 to March 20.

STAR STORY

The word "zodiac" comes from an ancient Greek phrase that means "circle of animals." Many of the signs of the zodiac, including Pisces, are animals.

THE ZODIAC IS DIVIDED INTO 12 SIGNS BASED ON CONSTELLATIONS.

IS THE SUN MOVING?

Throughout the course of one year, it seems as if the sun moves along a circular path around Earth called the ecliptic. During the year, the ecliptic seems to take the sun through all 12 constellations of the zodiac, including Pisces. Each month, the sun appears to move through a different constellation, which is why there are 12 constellations in the zodiac.

However, the sun isn't actually moving through the zodiac. Instead, the Earth's orbit, or path, around the sun is what makes it look like the sun is moving around Earth.

STAR STORY
The orbits of the other planets also exist within the circle of the ecliptic.

DIFFERENT CONSTELLATIONS ARE SEEN AT DIFFERENT TIMES OF THE YEAR BECAUSE OF EARTH'S ORBIT AROUND THE SUN.

SPRINGTIME IN PISCES

When the sun appears to move through Pisces along the ecliptic, it reaches the vernal equinox. We know the date it reaches the vernal equinox by another name, too: the first day of spring. This occurs each year around March 21.

An equinox is a point where the sun's path along the ecliptic crosses the celestial **equator**. The celestial equator is an imaginary line that represents Earth's equator extended into space. The vernal equinox marks the first day of spring in the Northern Hemisphere. The autumnal equinox marks the first day of fall, which occurs around September 21 each year.

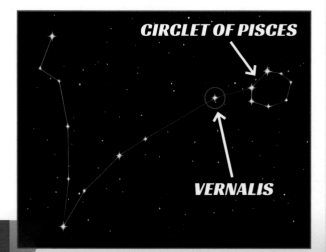

CIRCLET OF PISCES

VERNALIS

STAR STORY

One of the stars near the Circlet of Pisces is named Vernalis after the vernal equinox.

THE VERNAL EQUINOX, WHICH MARKS THE FIRST DAY OF SPRING, OCCURS WHEN THE SUN APPEARS TO REACH A POINT ALONG THE ECLIPTIC NEAR THE CIRCLET OF PISCES.

MEASURING MAGNITUDE

If you spend time stargazing and studying the stars, you'll notice that every star is slightly different. Two ways stars can be described are by their color and brightness.

Star color relates to how hot or cold a star is. A blue star is very hot, while a red star is the coldest a star can be. A star's brightness, which is measured in magnitude, also sets it apart from other stars. Stars with low magnitude numbers are the brightest. Polaris, which is also known as the North Star, has a magnitude of 2. The brightest star in Pisces has a magnitude of 3.6. That's a higher magnitude, which means it's not very bright.

STAR STORY
The brightest star in Pisces is sometimes called Eta Piscium.

ASTRONOMERS, OR PEOPLE WHO STUDY OBJECTS IN SPACE, HAVE BEEN USING MAGNITUDE TO MEASURE STAR BRIGHTNESS SINCE ANCIENT TIMES.

NAMING THE STARS

Some stars in constellations are given names based on the myth behind the constellation. For example, the star that marks the point of the V in Pisces is sometimes called Alrescha, or Alrisha. This name comes from the Arabic word for "the cord." The Arabic language was spoken by ancient astronomers from the Middle East who studied the stars in Pisces.

Another star in Pisces is named Van Maanen's Star after Adriaan van Maanen, who was the astronomer who discovered the star in 1917. It's one of the closest stars to Earth. It's also the closest white dwarf star to the sun.

STAR STORY
Van Maanen's Star is a very old star. White dwarves are some of the oldest stars in the sky.

VAN MAANEN'S STAR

ALRESCHA

ALRESCHA IS A DOUBLE STAR. A DOUBLE STAR IS A PAIR OF STARS THAT ARE VERY CLOSE TOGETHER AND ORBIT AROUND A COMMON CENTER.

STUDYING M74

When astronomers look at Pisces, they can see an entire galaxy named M74 in the constellation. A galaxy is a group of millions or billions of stars. The name M74 comes from the man who discovered this galaxy, Charles Messier. He made a **catalog** of the space objects he found in the sky before his death in 1817. M74 was the 74th object he found.

M74 is a kind of galaxy known as a spiral galaxy. A spiral galaxy looks like a pinwheel. M74 is made up of around 100 billion stars.

STAR STORY
M74 can be seen just outside of the V shape of Pisces near Eta Piscium.

M74 HAS REGIONS IN IT WHERE NEW STARS ARE FORMED. THESE REGIONS GIVE OFF A GLOW THAT CAN BE SEEN IN THIS PHOTO.

FINDING THE FISH

Pisces is one of the largest constellations. However, it's often hard to see in the sky with just our eyes because its stars aren't very bright. Many people look at Pisces and other constellations through telescopes. These tools make space objects appear larger. High-powered telescopes are used to study space objects that are very far away, such as M74.

If you want to look for Pisces, try to go stargazing in an area away from man-made lights. Bring an adult with you, and get ready to have fun looking for the fish in the sky!

GLOSSARY

catalog: A complete list of items with details.

cord: A long, thin rope used to tie or connect things together.

determine: To decide.

equator: An imaginary circle dividing the surface of a body into two equal parts. Earth's equator divides the planet into the Northern and the Southern Hemispheres.

hemisphere: Half of Earth.

myth: A story told in ancient cultures to explain a practice, belief, or part of nature.

personality: The set of emotional qualities and ways of behaving that make a person different from other people.

planet: A large, round object in space that travels around a star.

region: A broad area.

INDEX

WEBSITES

Due to the changing nature of Internet links, PowerKids Press has developed an online list of websites related to the subject of this book. This site is updated regularly. Please use this link to access the list: www.powerkidslinks.com/tcc/pisc